The Book of Were

By the same author

Man in a Window, 1965 (Coach House Press)
Eighteen, 1966 (Coach House Press)
For Everyone, 1967 (Fleye Press)
Music for the Words, 1967 (privately printed)
The Machinery, 1967 (privately printed)
Alphabook, 1972 (Makework Press)
Glass/Passages, 1976 (Oberon Press)
An Ache in the Ear: 1966–1976, 1979 (Coach House Press)
The sea us (with bpNichol) (unpublished)
Mirages, 1996 (privately printed)
On Abducting the 'Cello, 2004

Wayne Clifford

The Book of Were

The Porcupine's Quill

Library and Archives Canada Cataloguing in Publication

Clifford, Wayne, 1944–
The book of were / Wayne Clifford.

ISBN-13: 978-0-88984-281-6
ISBN-10: 0-88984-281-7

I. Title.

PS8555.L535B66 2006 C811'.54 C2006-904470-8

1 2 3 4 • 08 07 06

Published by The Porcupine's Quill, 68 Main St, Erin, Ontario NOB 1TO.
http://www.sentex.net/~pql

Readied for the press by Tim Inkster.
Copy edited by Doris Cowan.

Represented in Canada by the Literary Press Group.
Trade orders are available from University of Toronto Press.

We acknowledge the support of the Ontario Arts Council and the Canada Council for the Arts for our publishing program. The financial support of the Government of Canada through the Book Publishing Industry Development Program is also gratefully acknowledged. Thanks, also, to the Government of Ontario through the Ontario Media Development Corporation's OMDC Book Fund.

Canada Council for the Arts Conseil des Arts du Canada

Canada

ONTARIO ARTS COUNCIL
CONSEIL DES ARTS DE L'ONTARIO

For all the puppies

I want to thank the several readers of and the audiences for the drafts of this collection. My thanks especially to Tim Inkster, who first suggested the project, and with patience assembled the illustrations, and to MJ Edwards, who encouraged the length of the versional way.

Adepted

The armadillo makes no qualms
in taking her creator's alms.
A skin of thickened keratin
is tent-roof under sun wherein
she curls up sow-bug snug.

An armadillo's most profound
Godzilla-rampant on a mound
of social and well-ordered life
that takes its lesson out of strife
borne of Great Tunneller's shrug.

Agnosticism gives no place
to any thirsting desert race.
No maker means no slaking might
explain a providence so slight
as keeps ant-eating smug.

The Wakeful Closet Door

A homonym can be revealing:
To bear's the verb nose-rung with feeling
we drag forth muzzled with despair
whenever fate lets out its mastiffs
whenever rigour baits its fresh stiffs
teasing them to prance.

The shuffling, snuffling, shifting bear
the shaman drew on wick-lit wall
by flicker and by hope might swear
recorded bear allows us all
the bear we want by chance,

for there's in us a womb-clasped fear
that wants held checked majestic bear,
the god-thralled, man-masked, changeling bear,
shackled to its dance.

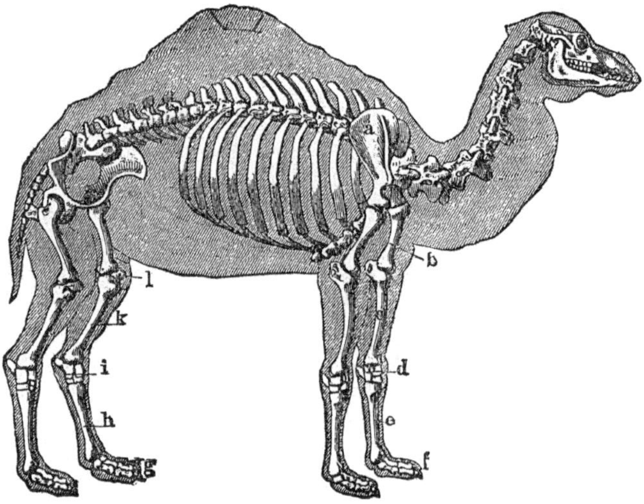
a
b
d
e
f
g
h
i
k
l

The Tides of Pampas

Camels used to sway thru pampas
burden-unencumbered,
invoked without a clock or compass
how the moon got numbered,
left, from croppings of the grass,
witness, beetle drovered.

Unchafed by these, our itchprick fears,
ungoaded by the why,
camels surveyed the pampal *heres,*
and chewed, and knelt, night nigh,
pampasination incomplete,
but perfectly.

If *we* pick out their bones from stone,
eyes down under intent sky,
our speculations stay our own,
not camels', pampasity.

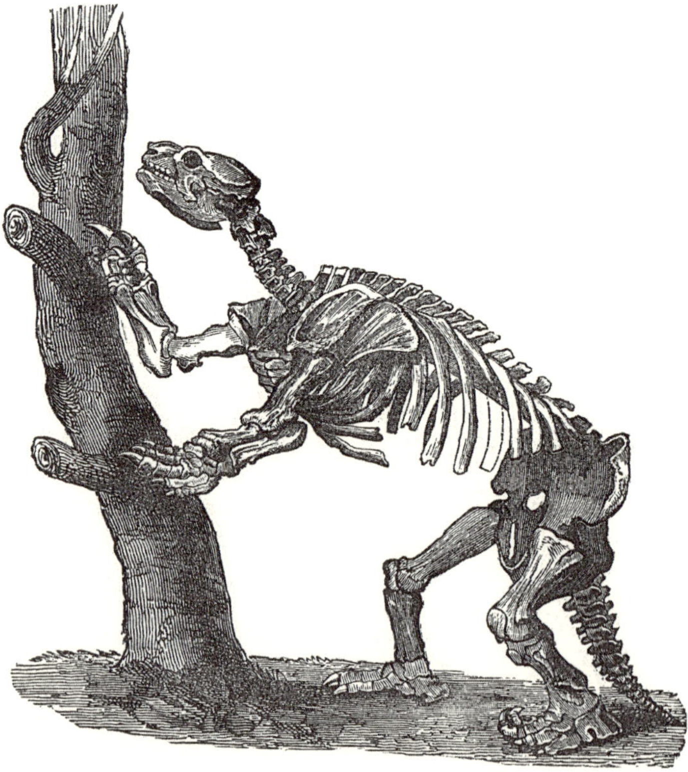

Masque

D is for Death.
Of all of God's beasts,
none other is fiercer;
none brings such release.
None else of God's creatures
so fills out God's grace,
for not one can offer
this singular prize:
Death's God's last monster
stares out from your eyes.

The Weight of Memory

The elephant knows of our need
nothing, perhaps, but what of greed
she comprehends by her own deed,

so as she's nudged by point to push
in piles the tangled roots as trash
before the burning turns them ash,
she only guesses at our wish.

For behemoth, neurons persist
in imaging the now-crushed cost
of goaded labour through the dust.

How then must hesitate that cause
to drag out any good at all
along the timber trail's strait laws,
when she can't use what she must pull?

A Japanese Tale

By bamboo grove, the fox folk come,
under the moon, the rice-white moon,
to yammer on their skin-tight drum,
under the powdered moon.

The tree alight with fireflies,
under the moon, the brow-shaved moon,
is no more final than foxes' lies,
under the old Noh moon.

The shamisen twangs out a tune;
the drum is battered to its ruin;
too soon the dream dissolves its koan
under the false-faced moon.

The Lesson

A few miles out of Orono,
a tired farm hid, going wild,
where we in boyhood summer'd go
to practise living hunting-wiled.

In its scrub-filling fields, we skilled
in up-stuck snout, for just below
bulked what secrecy we killed,
one true-aimed round from .22.

Pulled its mass up loose from hole,
hanged it, stiffening, our ghost
to bloat, sun-taunted, brag-told. Sold
the tail for two bits to our host.

The third day, roused the mess of flies
that'd queased a stink in tented sleep,
and came away, since world denies
to hold just body in its keep.

The Anatolian

He started Gandalf, ended Gandhi,
and venerable when he went.
He talked with me by what sound handy
got across just what he meant.

He'd been my eldest daughter's pet,
outgrown before his so long stay
embarrassed grade nine. As the debt
for having brought him first away

from pet store with his litter, wheel
and water bottle, pellet feed,
(for all my troubles, quite a deal)
I was who bought replacement stuff

and meeped back welcome getting home,
until, blind, bald, he'd had enough,
and left for plateaus hamsters roam
who have been good and true and kept.

And what he left, eared purse of skin,
which insignificance I wept
to lose such listener within.

After Their Trip to Guatemala, One Dines with One's In-Laws

'Tastes like chicken,' Max upheld,
'but it could have been the sauce.'
'Didn't like it,' Gina felt.
'Whole thing seemed a little gross.

'I mean, I'd seen them in the forest,
green and spiny, scuttling fast.
Well, *I* decided, to be honest,
just to make my breakfast last.'

'Ate her portion,' Max confided.
'Left the sauce, it was so hot!'
'Gave you heartburn,' Gina chided,
who'd fork her pot-roast, like as not.

Charm against Jaguar

Star-scroll-pelted
Underworld Lord,
You Who told Creators
breath and blood are sweet,
heed us under the paw of night

not yet.

Wave. Goodbye.

The hunting whale will herd them maw-
round, veiling bubbles up their clouds,
will cage them in a baleened jaw,
and lick down, blubber bound, their crowds.

The whale in Fundy summer mood
would rather herring, but our awe
to watch whale-breech's tourist proud.
Still, herring canned makes trading law.

Yes, we weired the catch allowed
(and shot the porpoise. No one saw.).
The day's soon here, that, frozen raw,
we'll ship out krill so we'll be owed.

The all god's given (and we're wowed)'s
enough to pay what well-fit shrouds
the best *men* win.
Do whales guffaw?

A Toast

On Madagascar, set adrift
these hundred million years by rift,
our species was as uncalled for
as man on moon, and thus Lemur
took over all the ape-rich niches.

In one of those chance-driven glitches
that seems so fated in hindsight,
our type arrived with enough might
more than a thousand years ago
to eat the slower lemurs, so

the fortune that the lemur can
revenge its race and dine on man
is shrinking fast as forest where
if we were lemurs swinging air-
ily, we'd gnaw that bitter rind,
despair, endemic to mankind.

We ghostly choruses would thrill
with hollow hoot, enchanted trill,
the probability that fable
might make our strong-jawed cousins able
better than did we to feel
the kill as blessing for the meal.

Lesson, moral, reason fail,
in column, comment, doggerel,
to push what haunted Malthus to
a point of caring. After you
are billions swarmed, resources bound,

leaving willingly for new found
homes, a little peace, some open
space. Folks, here's to hoping
a sermonizing so transparent
for a clan so unrepentant

out there somewhere might not find
that hunger powerful of mind
blind competition bets to breed
as counter to our apish greed.

A Dog's Lesson

Perseus once figured much on urn,
in painting, chipped from stone, his shield the forging
of your mortal grin that, past night's storm,
on a sobering beach, 's tumbled from the grey on-surging.

So out you're cast from your carousal-tangoed
waves and last night's love's that jellied thicket
you trail from your latest spasms. You envied sisters
their immortality but you in your so myriad

daughters, so long as sea keep salt, wave reach,
can, beached, sting the sniff of my nosy bitch.

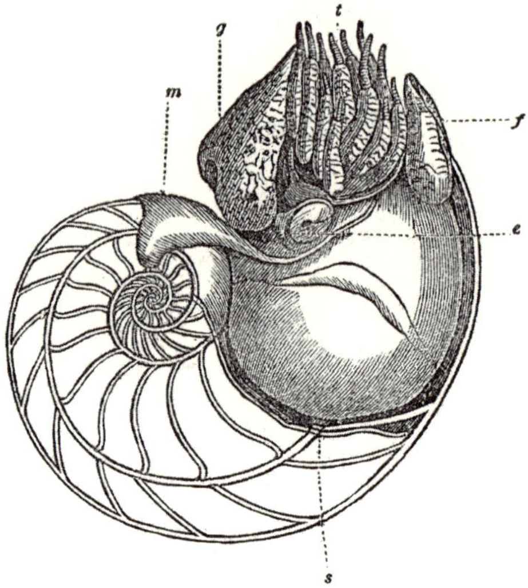
t
g
m
f
e
s

The Chamber

Deep, she secretes her suture-perfect curve
to gauge the month's gained more, slower days
as moon spirals away, faced in phase
that marks us, too.
                                        Just above, observe,
seafloor, she jets from extinction. Do we deserve
the shells in tens of thousands? Does our praise
raise the dead?
                                Doesn't the nacreous haze
of half-sawn backward tracing to spawn serve
our thirst for metaphor's dive down the salt well
to that point, naught in space-time,
                                                                Oz
in its unlit emerald heart, the precious glint
of secrets we're about to find out, the swell
of that great body a-sung in us, cause
of causes, of which an inner ear's the hint?

Aphrodisiac

The Book of Thomas wrote me joy
may lack completely but for trance
wherein one, holy, safely, and Thunder
da-da-dance.

                    The Who-makes-pearls-of-eyes-
and-other-irritants, whose burnished palace
burned no light as murked seas came and went,

fetching twenty bucks a kilo, not quite fresh
but neither bad, in that stentorian between,

oyster polishes her woe, assuming postures
antsy, bored, on crushed ice and on show.

Since the story knows the scribe, and scribe
knew glosses, since the ledges of our efforts,
and the shucking of our losses, Thomas

taught me incantatory faith can pull
from very air the stair.

                              But oyster,
plush as successful lust, has no derrière
(from French, whom Thomas was converting).
Behovable, it feeds where it secretes.

The French, whose sensitivity to speech
Thomas drew his strength from, raise
as answer sterner, older stuff. Their women
(Oh, the salt-taste *is* the oyster's face!)

and men knotted in one succulence
know oysters, bidden to the feast,
bear that glow of much abandoned
goddess so

                    scholars scratching thru middens
can estimate from shell-counts
the legion of Love's chosen
chained to hell-mounts.

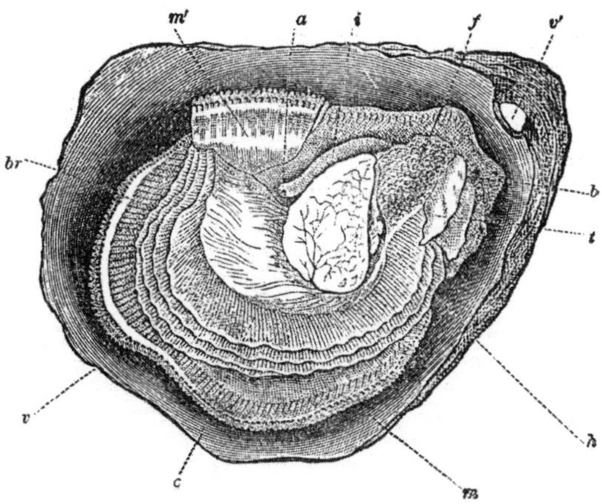

Thorny Answer

Spine pig, spine pig, say me true,
how your flesh befits a *you*
so articulate in joint
as to sharpen to your point.

I've kept dogs ten thousand days;
dodge my fears and play my joys
out there in the forest's maze,
as do totem-goaded boys.

Chewed my handle, yes, you have;
swollen snout to dog you'd give
who'd remonstrate with you about
the right to chew my saltsweat out.

Just as willful as some god
small- and mean-eyed, vengeful, odd,
taking what you want of mine,
impaling dog-law on a spine,

pig of pine, daemon of spruce,
if *you* make Zion, what's the use?

The Genome Project's Appeal to the NRA

One study has suggested the quagga might be bred back from zebra DNA, and that licences to hunt a selected cull of the subsequent stock might finance such a project.

The quagga hides as almost ghost
potential in its DNA,
and makes the 'pataphysic boast
that virtuality's okay.

The farmer on the voortrek veldt
saw this meat-chance on the hoof,
and fast as he could tan a pelt,
the quaggal history went *poof!*

Now some say we should breed it back
to rectify such boorish greed
as can descend from Boer attack
which kills more quadruped than we'd,

but, me, I'm truly buffaloed
when I'm told from some ass's seed
we'll get back what we're rifle-owed
so we can hunt the reclaimed breed.

Neighbours

The rat's a cunning critter,
a type surviving well.
While very few are fitter,
since evolution's cruel
and has for god a quitter,
the rat's no kind of fool,
and, litter after litter,
nibbles near her goal
of being heavy hitter
among her cladal whole.

What makes this biter bitter
is dealing with the bull
that man's the only glitter
in wide creation's jewel.
Not *know* but *gnaw*'s the matter
that warrens cellars full.

Fastidiously better
for primate's urban sprawl,
since, down streets residential,
the lights so softly fall,
rat yet might be begetter
of winner taking all.

How Sin Evolves

The medieval catalogue of character defects
was meant to drag man's dialogue up near where God expects,
until America's analogue brought home the sin's effects.

The sloth proves neither strifeful brute, nor sanguine, but sincere.
The problem of so slow a life is simply being here.
Since sleep can make the stay more brief, the less there needs to fear.

So blessed be sloth, the mossy beast, who's camouflaged in grace,
that even when he's shot beneath, his claws hold him in place;
his vision upwards thus bequeaths suspension of God's face.

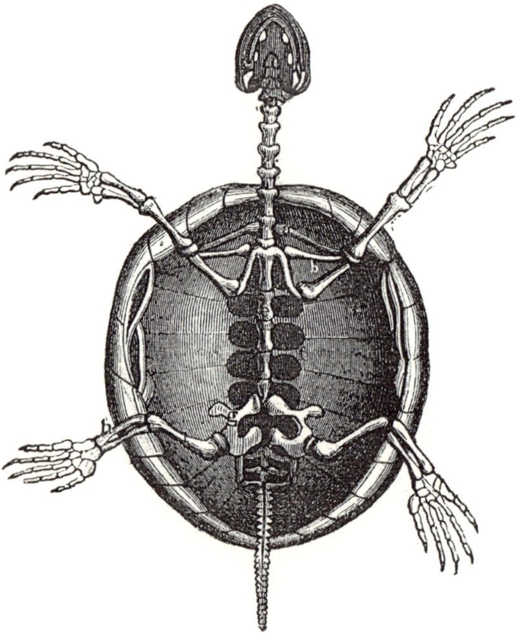

Galapagos

Its salty border utter law,
an island breeds from narrow genes,
and fills its niches, beak and claw,
by what deterministic means
can keep the possible as raw
as will allow for chance's liens.

Perhaps from tangled wood-mat's drift
your forebear waded up what shores
had upheaved from a magmic rift
so she could wander them on fours,
and contemplate how sacred gift
is learnt by nipping green-sharp stores.

The fourteen clans of tortoise thus,
from dry to moister, grew to own
the archipelago, no fuss,
and never thought the sea'd condone
self-righteous business such as us.
Offences? Soup. Defences, none.

In tortoise, time's the oddest verb,
its middle pinched into the draw
its long ends tangle from absurd:
that we, whose god's a moment's awe,
tour to see what Darwin saw.

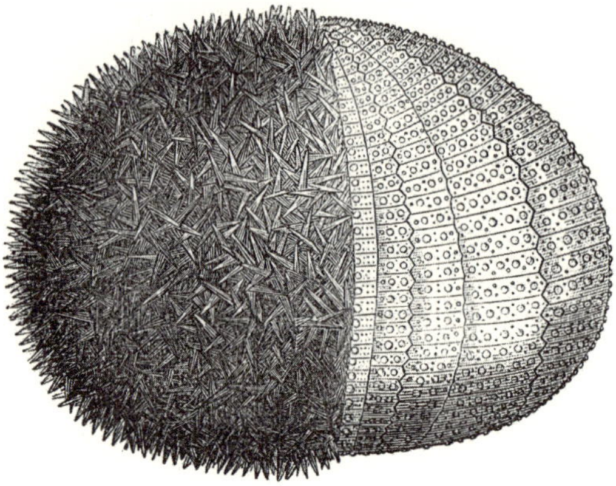

Sand Bowls

I come upon her emptinesses tide
has thrown, plundered shells. Past swell break,
bottom dark, her clan pock weed, and take
the pillages they can of gulls, died.
The corrugated muck, when tides subside,
shows written how the whelk awakes to stake
out curlicues about bleached pieces. Fake
sentiment will nowise make her tied
to anything I know of appetites,
nor let me see why, for her, the lights
of sun and moon are what the current writes
in milt and scent moved by their far thoughts.
The backwash drags the cobbles, which force allots
illusion: life-scuttle in her broken noughts.

Personae

Coyote loveth vole,
and pranceth midst the grass
and chomp thee, fellow, whole,
un(k)nick(er)ing tiny ass,

lets run upon his tongue
small clawpricks and thin tail,
until he's nipped among
his flewpoints, and nips skull.

O vole of little mass,
as tasty as the spring
which lengthens out the grass
so you may hide within,

Coyote loves you best
of locust, mouse or mole,
and grins a lip-smacked zest
at how you play your role.

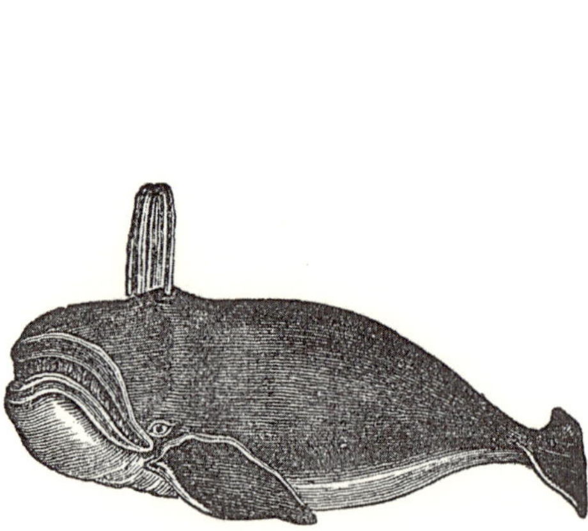

Turbulence

I'm whale and I dream. I fly water, for air's
where birds and monsters gather. The sea's thick
in squeak and echo and the krill rise quick
caged in my columned breath. My daughters' airs
are sung from love, unpublished poetesses
of the great depth darkening below us. Rock
is far and not sought but by the sick.
The dream's upheld and goes on beyond rest.

God gave me the sea and all in it.
I am Her first among the fishes and though
Shark follow, this plenty I inhabit
sounds to Her being's limit; She is the flow
in whom sink the dead. I dream. I know
I'm man elsewhere, held up by a bed.

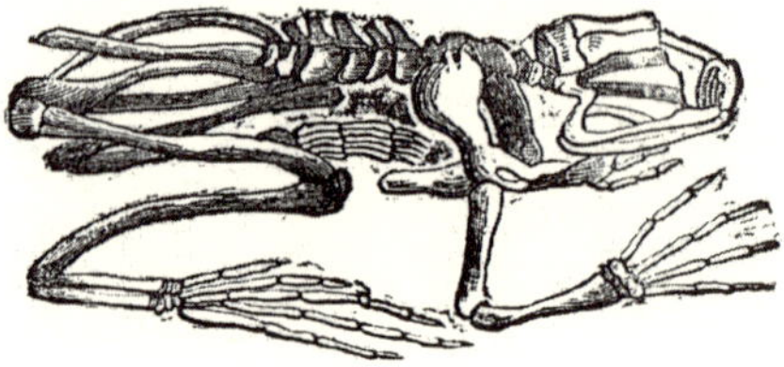

Embryonic Angels?

The only frog to date in space
was put up by our human race
to give frog cells a harder taste
of gamma radiation.

Our own genes will not so unmend
as xenopus's; to that end,
we sent a research team to tend
the first freefall mutation.

Which asks the question: just who dares,
if what we'll meet the months to Mars
and on from there years to the stars
may be transfiguration?

Before the Mystery's Gone

Hillary's party met no yeti
higher up the slopes.
Tenzing Norgay kept his counsel;
Hillary kept up hopes
and went back in '60
with trip-wire cameras.

No proof yet of Rock Beast,
yah teh, Sherpa words.
No Vengeance Thundering Down
the Mountain or other gods.
No old man full lotus frisky,
no demons, no chimeras.

No telling if we'll ever know.
The unknown by its nature
walks uprooting rhododendrons
in an alpine pasture,
bipedal, having chosen, risky,
that lonely calm, instead of us.

Tenzing spoke seven languages,
Yetish not among 'em.
Since hymns in Yetish aren't transcribed,
we don't know how who've sung 'em
might have sounded, though there must be

yetis calling, at times amorous
to plan the outcomes of the clan,
despite the pooh-poohings of man
at the passing of the chance
to be media glamorous.

Sacred Photosynthesis

The zebu's line goes back so far,
the god bedecked its neck for war,
and, blue-skinned, rode with (s)word to slay
illusion's everyday.

The god clove hoof and anger, broke
the willfulness of might on yoke,
so what regret huffs haltered snout
inspires in man insulted doubt
about a master's right.

For all man-pacts the ox has made,
the dancing god poses the same:
if one blue fist upraises blade,
one keeps still flame.

Scoff-god man, twister of ropes,
who bets so much on deathbed hopes,
can't hear which hymn played by the flute
astride the hump makes ox seem mute
that talks with god the moooncast night,

but flicked ear hears how jabs the goad
that grows the grass, nor thinks it odd
the wind eats chaff. The god as grain
laughs of fate the proof is man
and greens delight of light.

MARY JOAN EDWARDS

Wayne Clifford began writing at fourteen, and was first published at sixteen in *Fiddlehead.* At twenty, he published the founding collection with Coach House Press. In 1967, he shared the E. J. Pratt prize with Michael Ondaatje, and soon after was invited to the Writers' Workshop at the University of Iowa where he worked with Harry Duncan of Cummington Press in the School of Journalism, designing and laying out the award-winning *Iowa Review,* and teaching book design and production. He was an invited participant to the founding conference of the League of Canadian Poets in Toronto in 1968. Although he has never allied with a movement, group or school, he's collaborated with writers and artists as various as bpNichol, Vic D'Or, Allen Flint, Toby Andersen and the Monday Night Boys. During the seventies, eighties and nineties, much of his energy went into raising four children, and teaching language skills at a college in Kingston, Ontario. During this period, he explored the visual and musical arts, painting, drawing, and inventing several instruments which he then taught himself to play, but published very little, until the Porcupine's Quill released *On Abducting the 'Cello,* which received critical notice and sparked the interest of a new generation of writers. He presently writes full-time in Halifax.